WILD·WORLD·OF

LAKES AND RIVERS

MICHAEL CHINERY

ILLUSTRATED BY WAYNE FORD AND ERIC ROBSON

Kingfisher Books

Kingfisher Books, Grisewood & Dempsey Ltd,
Elsley House, 24–30 Great Titchfield Street,
London W1P 7AD

First published in 1992 by Kingfisher Books

British Library Cataloguing-in-Publication Data.
A catalogue record for this book is available from
the British Library

ISBN 0 86272 884 3

Series editor: Mike Halson
Series designer: Terry Woodley
Designer: Dave West Children's Books
Illustrators: Wayne Ford (pp. 1, 10–12, 15–17, 20–21,
26–28, 30–31, 36–37); Eric Robson (pp. 2–9, 13–14,
18–19, 22–25, 29, 32–35, 38)
Cover illustrations: John Butler

Phototypeset by Southern Positives and Negatives
(SPAN), Lingfield, Surrey.
Printed and bound by Cambus Litho Ltd, East Kilbride.

Contents

Life in the lakes and rivers

Most of the rain that falls on the land runs into rivers and flows down to the sea. Rivers usually start in the hills and mountains, because that is where most of the rain falls. An upland stream is narrow and fast. Other streams join it lower down and the river gets wider. It slows down as it reaches the flatter ground of the lowlands. Eventually it reaches the estuary and flows out to sea. Each region of the river has different kinds of plants and animals. The river shown here is typical of regions with a mild climate.

DO YOU KNOW

Waterfalls usually occur where rivers flow from hard rocks on to softer ones. The running water wears the softer rock away more quickly and leaves the hard rock standing up like a cliff with the river crashing noisily over it.

A lake forms where a river flows down into a hollow area. The river eventually finds its way out and continues its journey to the sea. All kinds of fish live in the lake and ospreys hunt them from the air. Grebes and other water birds live around the water's edge.

Grebe

Mountain streams are cold and rocky and are usually too fast for fish to live in them. Further down the valley the current is slower, and this is where the salmon comes to lay its eggs. Sticklebacks swim here too, and dippers nest along the water's edge.

Salmon

The stretch of river nearest the sea is called the estuary. The water is salty here. Flocks of wading birds visit the muddy banks uncovered at low tide to feed on worms and shell-fish. Otters hunt for eels and other fish in quiet estuaries.

Otter

The river flows slowly through the lowlands in great loops. Eels and many other fish swim here, but they are not easy to see in the muddy water. Swans nest on the river banks, while dragonflies dart through the air.

Dragonfly

DO YOU KNOW

The animals that live in the calm or still waters of lakes and ponds are similar to those of slow-moving rivers. Frogs and newts breed there in the spring, and so do ducks and moorhens.

The heavy hippopotamus

The hippopotamus is the world's biggest freshwater animal. It weighs up to 4 tonnes and, although it is a plant-eater, it is a very dangerous creature. An adult hippopotamus can pick up a crocodile and bite it in half. Hippos live in groups in and around the rivers of Africa. The adults have no enemies, but crocodiles often eat baby hippos. When people killed the crocodiles in one area the hippo population grew so much that they ate all the crops!

HIPPO FACTS

● Hippopotamus means 'river horse', but the hippo is actually a huge pig, up to 4 metres long and about 1.5 metres high. The male's tusks can be over 1 metre long.

● An adult hippo will eat about 200 kg of grass and other plants in a single night.

Male hippos fight with their tusks, which can cause terrible injuries. The hippos often die from their wounds.

Hippos come out of the water to graze on land at night. They often destroy farm crops. They also eat lots of water plants.

Oxpeckers commonly perch on hippos on the river bank. They eat the blood-sucking ticks and flies that attack the hippos.

? DO YOU KNOW

The hippo's skin is kept clean by a type of small fish. The fish even cleans the hippo's teeth for it.

The hippo can walk or run along the river bed for over 4 minutes without having to come up for air.

When resting in the river by day, the hippopotamus leaves just its eyes, ears and nostrils above the water.

The pond skater

The pond skater is an insect that lives on the surface of ponds and slow-moving streams. It rows itself across the water with its long middle legs and preys on small insects that fall on to the surface.

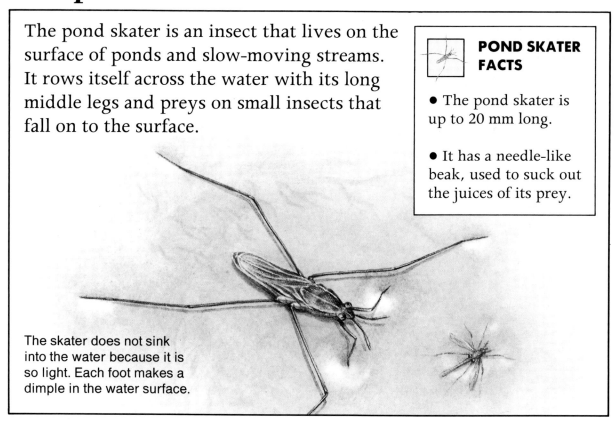

The skater does not sink into the water because it is so light. Each foot makes a dimple in the water surface.

The cunning raft spider

The raft spider spends most of its time on the surface of small pools. It usually rests on a floating leaf or twig. When the spider feels the vibrations of an insect or a small fish, it darts off to catch and eat it.

SURVIVAL WATCH

Raft spiders almost died out in Britain when the swamp that was their home began to dry up. New pools were dug to save them.

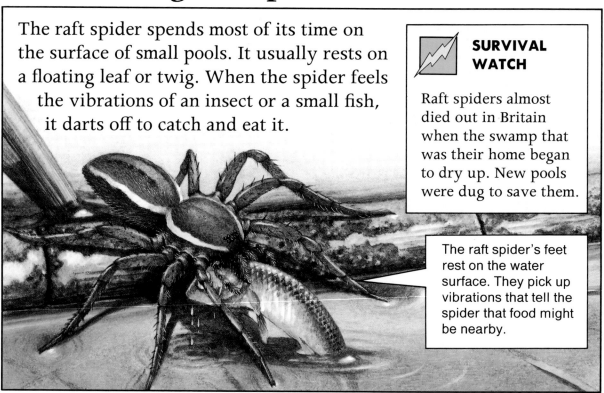

The raft spider's feet rest on the water surface. They pick up vibrations that tell the spider that food might be nearby.

The ever-hungry dipper

The dipper gets its name from its habit of bobbing up and down while standing on rocks in fast-flowing streams. It also spends up to two hours every day walking or swimming under the water. It eats all kinds of small water creatures, but freshwater shrimps are its favourite food. Dippers can be seen by upland rivers in many parts of the Northern Hemisphere. They nest among waterside rocks and trees.

DIPPER FACTS

● Dippers are 18 cm long and weigh about 75 grams. They can eat their own weight of food in a day.

● Dipper chicks can dive and swim before they can fly.

The dipper's eyes are specially constructed so that the birds can see just as well in the water as they can in the air.

The dipper often runs along the stream bed as it searches for food. It can also swim very well by flapping its wings.

The busy beaver

Beavers live by rivers in the forests of North America and Europe. They are wonderful builders and are famous for the dams that they build across streams. They usually build their homes, called lodges, in the ponds that form behind the dams. There they are safe from most of their enemies. Some beavers live in burrows in the river bank instead of in lodges, but the burrows still have underwater entrances. Beavers live in family groups of about 12 animals, and all the animals help with the work.

The lodge is built with sticks and mud. It has several underwater entrances, but the living space is above the water line. The beavers stay warm and dry there, even in the winter.

The dam is made from branches, stones, and mud. The beavers are always working on it to keep it in good condition.

Lodge

Dam

Entrance

Entrance

BEAVER FACTS

- The beaver is 130 cm long from nose to tail and weighs 30 kg. Its back feet are webbed for swimming.

- When a beaver spots an enemy, such as a wolf or a puma, it slaps the water with its tail. The sound can be heard up to 1 km away and it warns other beavers of the danger.

Beavers are strong swimmers and can stay underwater for 15 minutes. Dense, oily fur keeps their bodies dry and warm.

Beavers cut down trees with their sharp teeth. They eat the tender young shoots and use the rest to build with.

The broad tail is used for steering in the water. On land, it forms a sort of seat while the beaver gnaws the trees.

11

The air-breathing lungfish

Several kinds of lungfish live in tropical rivers. Their gills are not very efficient and they surface now and then to gulp air into simple lungs. Some lungfish drown if they can't get to the surface. Scientists think that some kinds of lungfish left the water millions of years ago and developed into the first newt-like amphibians. Lungfish feed mainly on water snails, which they crush with big flat teeth.

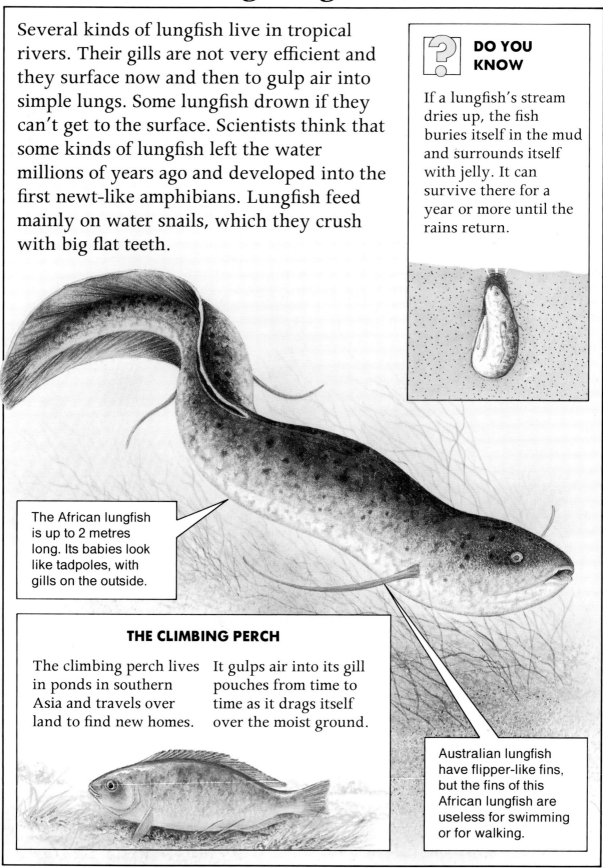

DO YOU KNOW

If a lungfish's stream dries up, the fish buries itself in the mud and surrounds itself with jelly. It can survive there for a year or more until the rains return.

The African lungfish is up to 2 metres long. Its babies look like tadpoles, with gills on the outside.

THE CLIMBING PERCH

The climbing perch lives in ponds in southern Asia and travels over land to find new homes. It gulps air into its gill pouches from time to time as it drags itself over the moist ground.

Australian lungfish have flipper-like fins, but the fins of this African lungfish are useless for swimming or for walking.

The sharp-shooting archer fish

The archer fish shoots at insects sitting on leaves hanging over the water. It can spot small flies as much as 2 metres above the surface, and knocks them down with a stream of water droplets fired from its mouth. The fish then snaps them up and eats them. The archer fish is about 30 cm long.

ARCHER FISH FACTS

● The archer fish lives in shallow water close to the banks of rivers and estuaries in South-East Asia and northern Australia. It swims out to sea to lay its eggs, and the baby fish swim back to the rivers.

The mouth and tongue of the archer fish form a narrow tube, just like the barrel of a gun. Water is pumped along it at high speed from the fish's throat and shoots into the air.

DO YOU KNOW

Young archer fish are not very good shots and they have to practise a lot before they get it right. Their aim and power get better as they grow up. An adult can send a jet of water up to 5 metres through the air.

The nest-building stickleback

Most fish simply scatter their eggs in the water, but the stickleback builds a cosy nest for its eggs. The father does all the work, and then guards the eggs and babies. The young fish leave when they are about two weeks old. If a baby swims away before this, the father dashes after it, grabs it in his mouth, and spits it back into the nest.

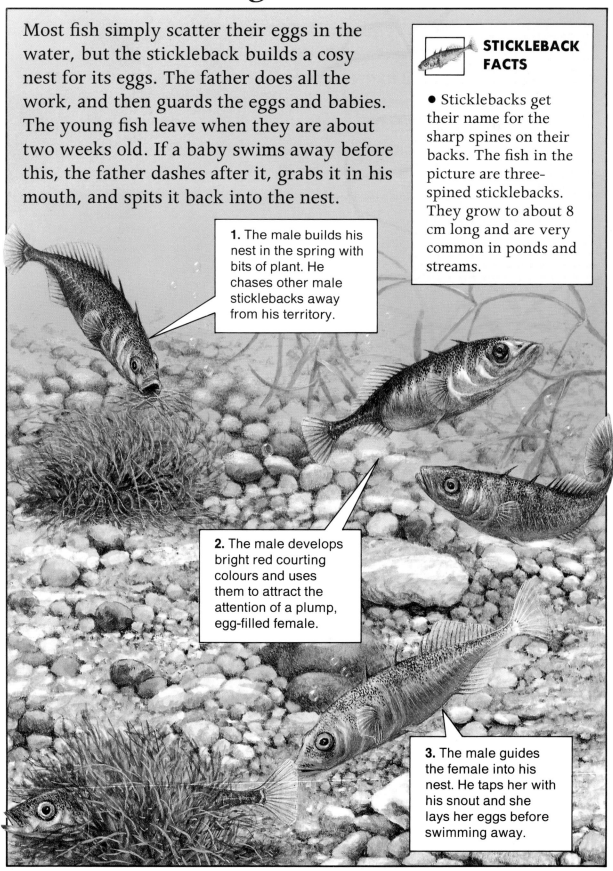

STICKLEBACK FACTS

● Sticklebacks get their name for the sharp spines on their backs. The fish in the picture are three-spined sticklebacks. They grow to about 8 cm long and are very common in ponds and streams.

1. The male builds his nest in the spring with bits of plant. He chases other male sticklebacks away from his territory.

2. The male develops bright red courting colours and uses them to attract the attention of a plump, egg-filled female.

3. The male guides the female into his nest. He taps her with his snout and she lays her eggs before swimming away.

The osprey

The osprey is a fish-eating bird of prey. It catches its fish in the sea as well as in fresh water. It can carry fish weighing over 1.5 kg – as heavy as the bird itself. Ospreys are great travellers and birds breeding in northern areas fly thousands of kilometres to spend the winter in warmer countries. They use the same treetop nests every year.

SURVIVAL WATCH

Ospreys have become rare birds in some places through people taking their eggs. Bird watchers have now started to guard the nest sites so the ospreys can rear their chicks in safety.

Broad wings provide the power necessary to lift a large fish into the air and to fly back to the nest with it.

Rough scales on the osprey's toes help them to get a good grip on a slippery fish as they snatch it from the water.

The adventurous salmon

The salmon spends much of its life in the sea, but it lays its eggs in the upper parts of rivers. Its journey up the river from the sea is long and dangerous and often involves leaping up waterfalls. The journey might take several months, but the salmon eats hardly anything during this time. Another amazing thing is that it always returns to the river in which it was born. Scientists think that it remembers the smell of its own river. Most salmon die after breeding, but some go back to the sea and may breed again.

SALMON FACTS

● Adult salmon are over 1 metre long and can weigh over 30 kg.

● European salmon often swim over 2000 km to Greenland, and spend up to four years in the sea before coming back to breed in their home rivers.

Salmon can jump as much as 3 metres out of the water and can easily leap over small waterfalls as they travel upstream.

A SALMON GROWS UP

A baby salmon is called an alevin. It is born with its own supply of food in a special pouch.

When it is about a year old, the young salmon gets red spots on its sides and is called a parr.

At about 15 cm long, the fish becomes a silvery smolt. It is now ready to go down to the sea.

Alevin

Parr

Smolt

Salmon usually reach their breeding areas in late summer. The males are bright red by this time.

The male salmon develops a strongly hooked jaw in the breeding season.

The female lays her eggs in a hollow, which she makes by flicking gravel away with her tail.

The long-legged flamingo

The flamingo is a really weird bird. It is up to 130 cm high and seems to be all legs and neck. It lives in shallow, muddy lakes and feeds with its head completely upside-down. Flamingos live in warm areas and are most common in Africa. Thousands of them live together in enormous pink flocks. Their nests are made of mud and look just like round cakes. Each nest has a single egg sitting in a hollow on the top.

The flamingo always flies with its neck straight and its long legs trailing behind. It looks rather like a colourful glider.

Flamingos get their delicate colour from the red pigments in the little shrimps that they eat.

The flamingo is very good at balancing on one leg. Its legs are so thin that the bird often appears to be floating in mid-air.

The flamingo catches shrimps and snails by sweeping its boat-shaped beak from side to side through the muddy water.

The big-beaked pelican

The pelican uses its huge beak like a bucket to scoop fish from the water. When it is fully expanded, the beak pouch can hold over 12 litres of water. White pelicans live on lakes in many parts of the world. They are a bit clumsy on land, but they are graceful swimmers and superb fliers. They nest on the ground or in low trees.

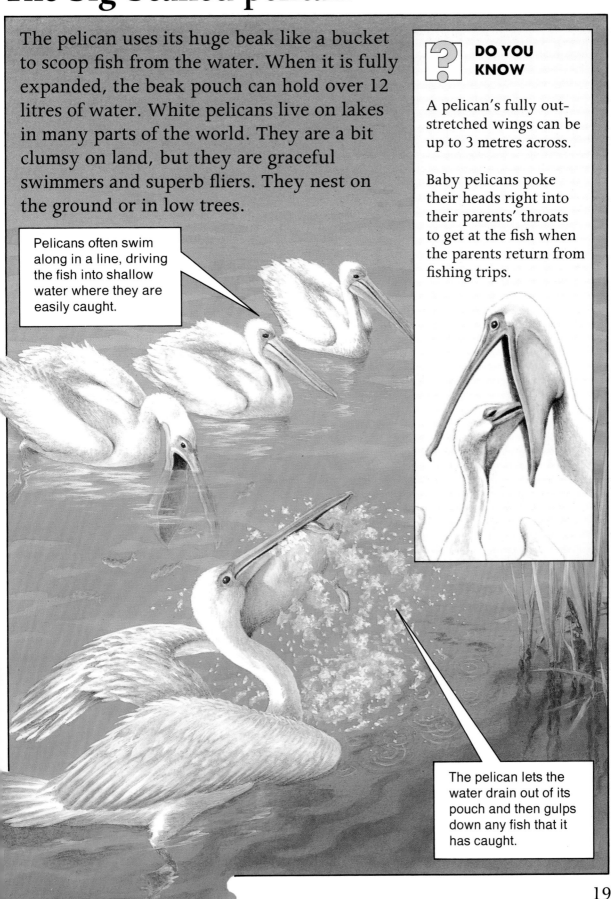

DO YOU KNOW

A pelican's fully out-stretched wings can be up to 3 metres across.

Baby pelicans poke their heads right into their parents' throats to get at the fish when the parents return from fishing trips.

Pelicans often swim along in a line, driving the fish into shallow water where they are easily caught.

The pelican lets the water drain out of its pouch and then gulps down any fish that it has caught.

The playful otter

Otters are water-loving cousins of the badger. They feed mainly on fish and leave piles of bones here and there on the river bank. The European otter pictured here is about 1 metre long. It makes its home in a hole in the river bank, where the female rears two or three cubs. Otters also live on the coast and catch fish in the sea.

SURVIVAL WATCH

Otters are rare animals. Fishermen used to kill them, and pollution has driven them from many rivers. Careful protection is helping them to increase again.

Otters are playful animals and they love to slide down muddy or snowy banks into the water.

The otter often uses its strong tail to prop itself upright. This helps it to see if any enemies are nearby.

A thick coat keeps the otter warm and dry even in the water. The water cannot get through the dense fur.

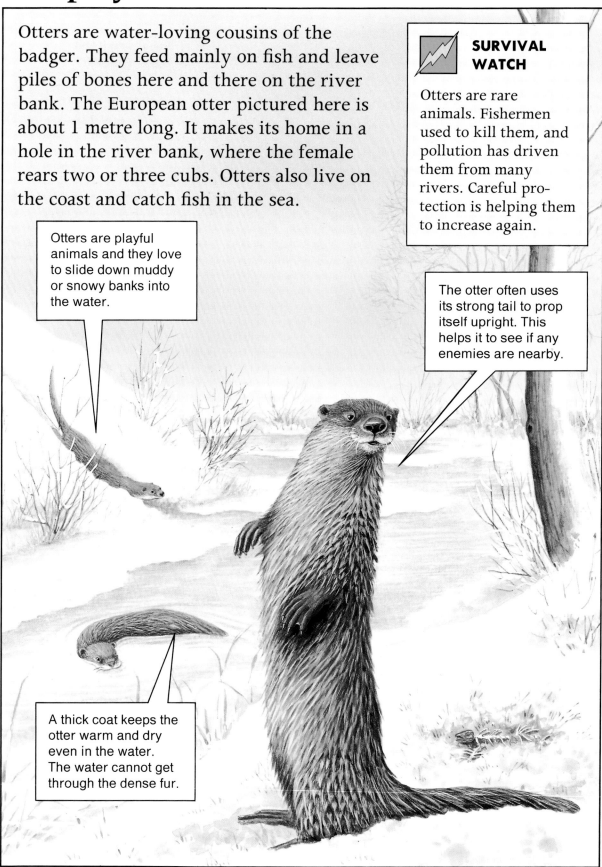

The meddlesome mink

The mink is famous for its fur, which is made into expensive coats. American mink have escaped from fur farms in Europe and have got themselves a bad name by killing all kinds of other wild animals and raiding poultry farms.

MINK FACTS

● Mink live in North America and Europe and are 50 cm long.

● American mink have the best fur and are reared on farms in many places.

The mink's feet are only partly webbed. It is a good swimmer, but not as good as its cousin the otter.

The coypu

The coypu is a large cousin of the rat and comes from the rivers and swamps of South America. Coypus were taken to Europe in the 1930s and reared for their fine fur. Many escaped and became pests because they damaged river banks and ate crops.

COYPU FACTS

● The coypu is about 1 metre long from nose to tail. Its soft fur is called nutria.

● Coypus swim well with the help of their webbed back feet.

The wandering eel

Eels are extraordinary fish. They are born way out in the middle of the Atlantic Ocean and drift thousands of kilometres to the rivers of North America and Europe. After a few years, when they are fully grown, they swim all the way back again to their birthplace. They do not eat on their long journey, and die soon after the eggs are laid.

EEL FACTS

● The eel grows to about 1 metre in length and weighs up to 3.5 kg.

● Eels eat frogs, fish, and other creatures, but can go without food for four years.

1. Baby eels are flat and transparent. They take from one to three years to drift across the ocean to the rivers where they will live. They are 7 cm long when they arrive.

2. When the babies reach the coast they change into pencil-shaped elvers about 6 cm long. They swim up the rivers and eventually turn into adult eels.

3. Adult eels can survive out of water for many hours. They often wriggle over land at night to reach new lakes or streams.

The stunning electric eel

The electric eel has special muscles that work like batteries. They send electric currents through the water to kill fish and other animals for food. The shocks can even kill people. Weaker currents act like radar signals to help the fish to find its way.

ELECTRIC EEL FACTS

● Electric eels are up to 3 metres long.

● They live in muddy South American rivers and are not related to true eels (see page 22).

The electric eel's eyes are small. Eyes are not of much use in the muddy water where the eel lives.

Ferocious piranhas

Piranhas live in the rivers of tropical America. They feed mainly on other fish, but their strong jaws and razor sharp teeth can quickly reduce almost any animal to a skeleton.

PIRANHA FACTS

● Some types of piranha are 60 cm long, but most are about 30 cm long.

● Amazonian Indians use piranha teeth as knives and scissors.

The piranha hunts by scent. It picks up the smell of its prey in deep pits in its snout.

The graceful swan

The swans shown here are mute swans, which live on ponds and slow-moving rivers in many parts of Europe and Asia. They weigh up to 18 kg and are among the heaviest of all flying birds. Once they have paired up, the male and female swans stay together for life. Their nest is an untidy pile of twigs and leaves built among the reeds or on the river bank. Swans feed mainly on plants, on land or in the water, but they also eat small fish and other water animals.

Mute swans have five or more babies, called cygnets, and they all stay together for several months. The cygnets do not become completely white until they are about two years old.

SURVIVAL WATCH

Many swans have died of lead poisoning after swallowing lead weights lost or thrown away by fishermen. Plastic weights are now being used and the swans are not being poisoned, but they still get tangled up in old fishing lines.

Feathers on the ground show where the adult swans have been moulting after the breeding season.

Because it is so heavy, the swan has to run across the water for perhaps 100 metres before it can get airborne.

Swans feed mainly on water plants. They often put their heads and necks right into the water to reach plants on the bottom.

? DO YOU KNOW

Whooper swans and Bewick's swans breed in the far north. They fly thousands of kilometres in order to spend the winter in warmer places.

Most swans are white, but the native swans of Australia are all black.

Black swan

The noisy moorhen

The moorhen lives on overgrown ponds and quiet streams. It looks a bit like a duck, but it does not have a flat beak. It is rather shy and is most likely to be seen swimming jerkily in and out of the reeds. When disturbed, it sounds its loud alarm call – *kuruk, kuruk* – to warn other birds. Moorhens often graze in waterside fields.

 DO YOU KNOW

The coot resembles the moorhen, but it has a white forehead. It also has a different call – *kook* instead of *kuruk* – but it is just as noisy as the moorhen.

Coot

The moorhen is not a strong flier. It has to run fast along the water surface before being able to take off.

Moorhens usually nest at the water's edge. The female lays about ten eggs. The chicks can swim when only a few hours old.

Moorhens' feet are not webbed. They cannot swim as well as ducks and spend a lot of time on land.

The dainty lily trotter

Lily trotters get their name because they walk on the floating leaves of water lilies and other plants. They are also called jacanas. This one is the comb-crested jacana from Australia and South-East Asia. The female jacana lays up to four shiny eggs in floating nests but it is the male who then looks after the eggs and the chicks.

LILY TROTTER FACTS

● There are seven kinds of lily trotter. Pheasant-tailed jacanas are the largest. They measure up to 50 cm from beak to tail.

● A frightened baby jacana often hides in its father's feathers.

The lily trotter's slender beak picks up insects and other small animals. The bird also eats some types of plants.

Long toes and claws spread the lily trotter's weight over several leaves, so it does not sink into the water.

The water spider

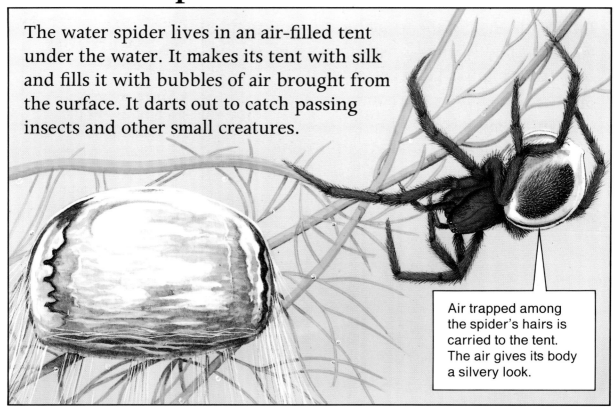

The water spider lives in an air-filled tent under the water. It makes its tent with silk and fills it with bubbles of air brought from the surface. It darts out to catch passing insects and other small creatures.

Air trapped among the spider's hairs is carried to the tent. The air gives its body a silvery look.

The great diving beetle

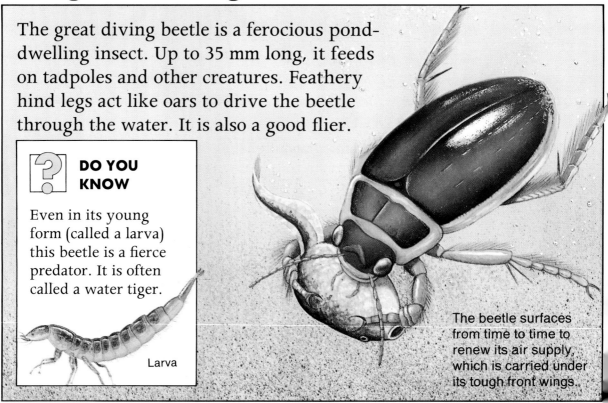

The great diving beetle is a ferocious pond-dwelling insect. Up to 35 mm long, it feeds on tadpoles and other creatures. Feathery hind legs act like oars to drive the beetle through the water. It is also a good flier.

? DO YOU KNOW

Even in its young form (called a larva) this beetle is a fierce predator. It is often called a water tiger.

Larva

The beetle surfaces from time to time to renew its air supply, which is carried under its tough front wings.

Speedy dragonflies

Dragonflies are among the world's fastest insects. They can zoom through the air at speeds of 30 km/h and can make amazing high-speed turns to snatch smaller insects in mid-air. Some can even hover and fly backwards. Many dragonflies have regular perches and dart off from time to time to grab passing insects.

DRAGONFLY FACTS

● There are over 5000 kinds of dragonflies. They are sometimes called horse-stingers, but they have no sting and are quite harmless.

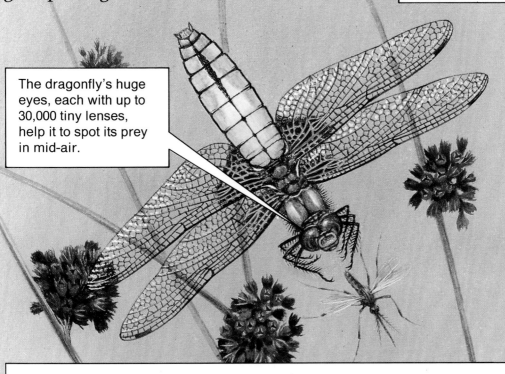

The dragonfly's huge eyes, each with up to 30,000 tiny lenses, help it to spot its prey in mid-air.

THE LIFE CYCLE OF A DRAGONFLY

1. Dragonflies lay their eggs in water, often while still in flight.

2. Young dragonflies, called nymphs, feed on small water creatures.

3. The nymph sheds its old skin and turns into an adult dragonfly.

The dancing newt

Like frogs and toads, the newt spends part of its life in the water and part on land. Newts eat lots of tadpoles and insects in the water. On land, they like damp places where they can find slugs and worms to eat. The newts shown here are warty newts, about 10 cm long.

In the mating season, the female is courted by the male. He shows off by dancing about in front of her, waving his colourful tail and crest.

DO YOU KNOW

Baby newts are called tadpoles. They live in water and breathe with feathery gills. After three months, the tadpoles lose their gills and leave the water. They now breathe with lungs.

Tadpoles

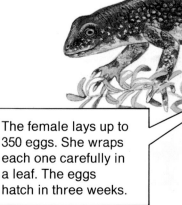

The female lays up to 350 eggs. She wraps each one carefully in a leaf. The eggs hatch in three weeks.

SURVIVAL WATCH

Newts are now rare in many places where old ponds have been filled in or have become overgrown. Making a garden pond will give the newts a home and help them to survive.

The Surinam toad

Surinam toads live in South America. When the eggs are laid, the male presses them into the female's spongy back. Each egg has its own covered pool in which it turns first into a tadpole and then into a miniature toad. Surinam toads rarely leave the water.

The axolotl – a big baby

The axolotl is a Mexican cousin of the newt, but it does not really grow up. It stays in the water and keeps its tadpole-like look all its life, but it can still mate and lay eggs. Axolotls are up to 15 cm long. They eat small fish and other water creatures.

The curious platypus

The platypus is one of Australia's strangest animals. It has a beak like a duck and a body like a beaver, and it lays eggs like a snake. Biologists thought it was a fake when they first saw a platypus skin, but the animal is real enough. It is about 50 cm long, with a dense fur coat and webbed feet. It lives in the rivers of eastern Australia and eats all kinds of small animals.

The platypus hunts mainly at night. It finds its food with its sensitive beak. Flaps of skin protect its eyes and ears under the water.

SURVIVAL WATCH

The platypus nearly died out in the 19th century because it was caught for its fine fur. When trapping was stopped, the platypus made an amazing recovery. It is no longer in any danger of extinction.

The platypus propels itself along using its webbed front feet. The tail and hind feet are used for steering.

The animal is often called the duck-billed platypus. Its long, rounded beak is very soft and rubbery and has no teeth.

DO YOU KNOW

The female platypus digs a burrow several metres long in the river bank. She lays up to three small, leathery eggs. She is a mammal and so feeds her babies on milk from her body.

Nest

Entrance

The great crested grebe

The great crested grebe gets its name for the eye-catching crest of feathers on its head in the breeding season. It swims, dives, and flies well, but it is rather clumsy on land because its legs are very far back and it can't balance very well. Grebes eat small fish and other water-dwelling animals. Their nests are piles of rotting leaves floating in the water.

GREBE FACTS

● The great crested grebe is 50 cm long.

● It lives on lakes and ponds in many parts of the world, but often spends the winter on the coast.

● It can swim under-water for up to three minutes, at speeds of over 10 km/h.

Male and female are alike. During court-ship, they dance around each other, with pieces of water plant in their beaks.

Baby grebes can swim as soon as they hatch from their eggs, but often ride on their parents' backs during the first few weeks.

The toothy crocodile

Crocodiles are the world's largest living reptiles and they are very dangerous creatures. Several different kinds live in and around the tropical rivers. The ones pictured here are Nile crocodiles from Africa. They feed mainly on fish, but the biggest ones catch the antelope and zebras that come to drink from the rivers. Their long jaws, armed with 66 teeth, quickly tear their victims to pieces.

 CROCODILE FACTS

● Crocodiles are up to 6 metres long. Some probably live for over 100 years.

● Crocodiles are the nearest living relatives of the great dinosaurs that roamed the Earth millions of years ago.

Crocodiles spend a lot of time sun-bathing. If they get too hot they move into the shade or slide into the water.

When floating in the water, crocodiles keep their eyes and nostrils just above the surface so that they can see and breathe.

? DO YOU KNOW

Crocodiles lay leathery eggs. Newly-hatched babies are about 30 cm long and the female carries them to a safe place. The babies live on land and feed mainly on frogs and insects. Later they move into the water and eat fish.

A crocodile usually slithers along on its belly, but it can also lift itself up on its legs and walk.

SURVIVAL WATCH

Crocodile skin shoes and handbags became popular about 100 years ago, and so many crocodiles were killed for their skins that they disappeared entirely from some areas. Trade in crocodile skin has now been banned, but many crocodiles are still being killed.

Plovers often enter crocodiles' mouths to peck blood-sucking leeches from their gums. The crocodiles don't harm the birds.

The dazzling kingfisher

The kingfisher fishes in shallow streams and pools in most parts of Europe and Asia. It usually fishes from a branch hanging over the water. Sticklebacks are its favourite food. They are swallowed whole when the kingfisher gets back to its perch. The bird has to turn them round in its beak and swallow them head first, so that their spines do not stick in its throat.

The kingfisher's eye contains droplets of red oil that act like sunglasses, so the bird is not dazzled by the bright water.

SURVIVAL WATCH

Many kingfishers die in cold winters because they can't fish in frozen streams. They also need clean water. Pollution has driven them from many rivers.

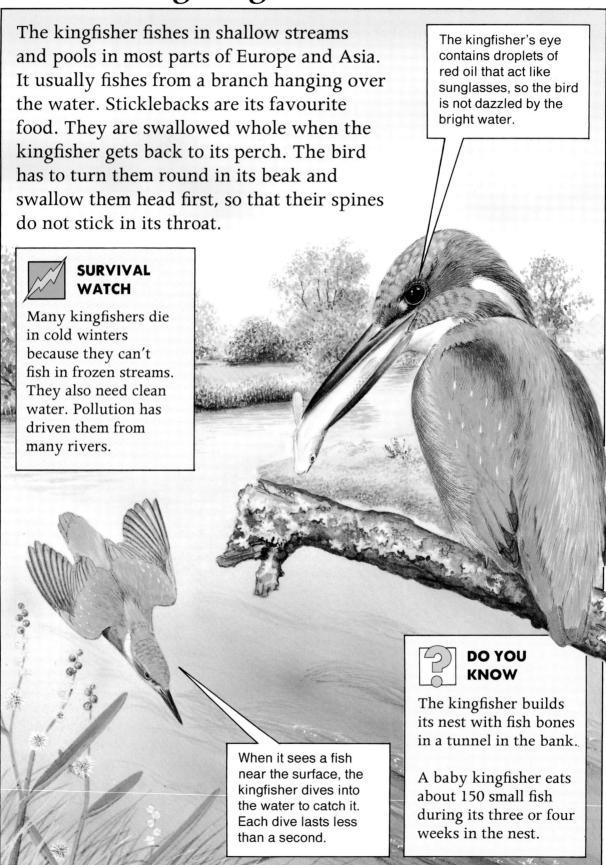

When it sees a fish near the surface, the kingfisher dives into the water to catch it. Each dive lasts less than a second.

DO YOU KNOW

The kingfisher builds its nest with fish bones in a tunnel in the bank.

A baby kingfisher eats about 150 small fish during its three or four weeks in the nest.

The patient heron

The heron is a patient fisherman. It catches fish and frogs in shallow water. After fishing, it cleans its feathers with its own dry shampoo, which it makes from small, crumbly feathers. Herons build their untidy nests close together in tall trees. They use the same trees year after year.

DO YOU KNOW

The African black heron uses its wings as a sunshade when it is hunting. The shadow helps it to see into the water. It may also attract fish right up to the bird's beak.

In flight, the heron bends its neck and pulls its head right back. It flaps its wings very slowly.

The heron often wades in the water to find food. It snatches up prey quickly in its long pointed bill.

A heron often stands for hours on one leg as it waits for prey. The head is usually pulled right down to the shoulders.

Rivers in danger

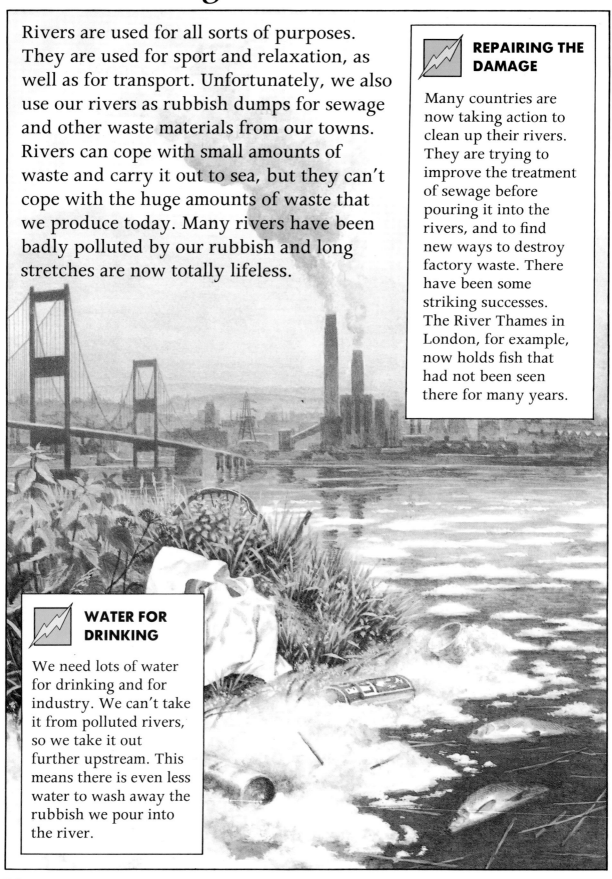

Rivers are used for all sorts of purposes. They are used for sport and relaxation, as well as for transport. Unfortunately, we also use our rivers as rubbish dumps for sewage and other waste materials from our towns. Rivers can cope with small amounts of waste and carry it out to sea, but they can't cope with the huge amounts of waste that we produce today. Many rivers have been badly polluted by our rubbish and long stretches are now totally lifeless.

REPAIRING THE DAMAGE

Many countries are now taking action to clean up their rivers. They are trying to improve the treatment of sewage before pouring it into the rivers, and to find new ways to destroy factory waste. There have been some striking successes. The River Thames in London, for example, now holds fish that had not been seen there for many years.

WATER FOR DRINKING

We need lots of water for drinking and for industry. We can't take it from polluted rivers, so we take it out further upstream. This means there is even less water to wash away the rubbish we pour into the river.

Useful words

Amphibian   An animal that spends its early life in water and then lives both in the water and on land. Frogs, toads and newts are amphibians.

Bird of prey   Any bird belonging to the hawk and eagle group of birds, with strong claws and a hooked beak. These birds feed on a wide range of other animals.

Breeding season   The time of year at which a particular kind of animal lays its eggs or has its babies.

Courtship   The process of attracting a mate. Animals often do this by showing off their bright colours.

Cub   The name given to the young of many meat-eating animals, including otters, foxes and bears.

Estuary   The lowest part of a river, close to where it meets the sea. The water here is slightly salty and the depth changes with the rise and fall of the tide.

Fin   Any of the limbs or other flaps which fish use for swimming. The fins are often very thin and delicate.

Flock   The name given to a group of birds, all of the same kind, that move about and feed together.

Freshwater   A freshwater animal is one that lives in the water of lakes and rivers and not in the salty water of the sea.

Gill   The breathing organ of fish and many other water animals. It takes oxygen from the water flowing over it.

Lung   The breathing organ of mammals and many other air-breathing animals. Oxygen passes from the air, through the thin walls of the lung, and into the animal's blood.

Mammal   Any animal that feeds its babies with milk from the mother's body. Most mammals are covered with fur, which helps to keep their bodies warm and at a steady temperature.

Moulting   The regular changing of the outer skin or coat. Birds often moult in the summer, when they replace their worn-out feathers with a new set.

Northern Hemisphere   That half of the world to the north of the Equator.

Pest   Any animal or plant that is a nuisance to people.

Pigment   Any substance that gives an animal or a plant its colour.

Pollution   The spoiling of water, air or soil with poisonous or harmful substances.

Prey   Any animal that is caught and eaten by another creature – the predator.

Swamp   An area of wet ground that has water lying on the surface nearly all the time.

Tadpole   The fish-like early stage in the life of a frog, toad or newt.

Tropical   To do with the tropics. These are the warm areas of the world on each side of the Equator.

Index